FRANCIS FRITH'S
TOWN & **CITY**
MEMORIES

ROMSEY

PAT GENGE, JESSICA SPINNEY & BARBARA BURBRIDGE
are long serving members of LTVAS Group, Romsey's local
history and archaeological society, which was founded in 1973.
The Group researches Romsey's history and has been responsible
for 16 books on various aspects of the history of the area. The
latest History of Romsey was published in 2000 and covers the
period from prehistory to the present day.

White Horse Hotel 1903 49340

FRANCIS FRITH'S
TOWN & CITY
MEMORIES

ROMSEY

PAT GENGE, JESSICA SPINNEY AND
BARBARA BURBRIDGE

FRANCIS FRITH'S
TOWN & CITY
MEMORIES

First Published as Romsey, A Photographic History of Your Town
in 2001 by Black Horse Books, an imprint of The Francis Frith Collection

Revised edition published in the United Kingdom in 2005 by
The Francis Frith Collection as Romsey, Town and City Memories

Limited Subscribers Hardback Edition 2005
ISBN 1-84589-014-0
Paperback Edition 2005
ISBN 1-85937-962-1

British Library Cataloguing in Publication Data

Romsey
Town and City Memories
Pat Genge, Jessica Spinney and Barbara Burbridge

The Francis Frith Collection
Frith's Barn, Teffont,
Salisbury, Wiltshire SP3 5QP
Tel: +44 (0) 1722 716 376
Email: info@francisfrith.co.uk
www.francisfrith.co.uk

Aerial photographs reproduced under licence from Simmons Aerofilms Limited
Historical Ordnance Survey maps reproduced under licence from Homecheck.co.uk

Printed and bound in England

Front Cover: **ROMSEY, MARKET PLACE 1904** 51431t
The colour-tinting in this image is for illustrative purposes only,
and is not intended to be historically accurate

FRANCIS FRITH'S
TOWN & CITY
MEMORIES

CONTENTS

F rancis Frith, Victorian founder of the world-famous photographic archive, was a devout Quaker and a highly successful Victorian businessman. By 1860 he was already a multi-millionaire, having established and sold a wholesale grocery business in Liverpool. He had also made a series of pioneering photographic journeys to the Nile region. The images he returned with were the talk of London. An eminent modern historian has likened their impact on the population of the time to that on our own generation of the first photographs taken on the surface of the moon.

Frith had a passion for landscape, and was as equally inspired by the countryside of Britain as he was by the desert regions of the Nile. He resolved to set out on a new career and to use his skills with a camera. He established a business in Reigate as a specialist publisher of topographical photographs.

Frith lived in an era of immense and sometimes violent change. For the poor in the early part of Victoria's reign work was a drudge and the hours long, and ordinary people had precious little free time. Most had not travelled far beyond the boundaries of their own town or village. Mass tourism was in its infancy during the 1860s, but during the next decade the railway network and the establishment of Bank Holidays and half-Saturdays gradually made it possible for the working man and his family to enjoy holidays and to see a little more of the world. With characteristic business acumen, Francis Frith foresaw that these new tourists would enjoy having souvenirs to commemorate their days out. He began selling photo-souvenirs of seaside resorts and beauty spots, which the Victorian public pasted into treasured family albums.

Frith's aim was to photograph every town and village in Britain. For the next thirty years he travelled the country by train and by pony and trap, producing fine photographs of seaside resorts and beauty spots that were keenly bought by millions of Victorians.

THE RISE OF FRITH & CO

Each photograph was taken with tourism in mind, the small team of Frith photographers concentrating on busy shopping streets, beaches, seafronts, picturesque lanes and villages. They also photographed buildings: the Victorian and Edwardian eras were times of huge building activity, and town halls, libraries, post offices, schools and technical colleges were springing up all over the country. They were invariably celebrated by a proud Victorian public, and photo souvenirs – visual records – published by F Frith & Co were sold in their hundreds of thousands. In addition, many new commercial buildings such as hotels, inns and pubs were photographed, often because their owners specifically commissioned Frith postcards or prints of them for re-sale or for publicity purposes.

In order to gain some understanding of the scale of Frith's business one only has to look at the catalogue issued by Frith & Co in 1886: it runs to some 670 pages. By 1890 Frith had created the greatest specialist photographic publishing company in the world, with over 2,000 stockists! The picture on the right shows the Frith & Co display board on the wall of the stockist at Ingleton in the Yorkshire Dales (left of window). Beautifully constructed with a mahogany frame and gilt inserts, it displayed a dozen scenes.

POSTCARD BONANZA

The ever-popular holiday postcard we know today took many years to appear, and F Frith & Co was in the vanguard of its development. Postcards became a hugely popular means of communication and sold in their millions. Frith's company took full advantage of this boom and soon became the major publisher of photographic view postcards.

Francis Frith died in 1898 at his villa in Cannes, his great project still growing. His sons Eustace and Cyril continued their father's monumental task, expanding the number of views offered to the public and recording more and more places in Britain, as the coasts and countryside were opened up to mass travel. The archive Frith created continued in business for another seventy years. By 1970 it contained over a third of a million pictures of 7,000 cities, towns and villages. The massive photographic record Frith has left to us stands as a living monument to a special and very remarkable man.

This book shows your town as it was photographed by this world-famous archive at various periods in its development over the past 150 years. Every photograph was taken for a specific commercial purpose, which explains why the selection may not show every aspect of the town landscape. However, the photographs, compiled from one of the world's most celebrated archives, provide an important and absorbing record of your town.

ROMSEY FROM THE AIR 1959 AFA74652

INTRODUCTION

I
n a guide book called 'The Beauties of England' published in 1762, Romsey is described thus: 'being situated in a Valley, and but few miles from the Sea, [it] is in the winter much subject to fogs and hazy weather; and the soil being somewhat greasy, it is vulgarly termed Romsey in the Mud. But since the Turnpike Roads are finished it is rendered much more agreeable, and the people live to considerable ages. The tradesmen in general live very comfortably, and though the number of Gentry is very small, the town is not without a genteel and well-managed Boarding School for Young Ladies. This place being so near the coast is much burthened with soldiers. Fish and Port Wine are cheap, but coals dear; the common people therefore burn peat, with which the valley abounds. On the different Streams of this valley are many mills for corn, paper, leather etc which turn to good account'.

The town has grown since that 18th-century traveller visited it; but its western boundary is still the River Test, and the Abbey is still the dominant building when the town is viewed from the hills on the west. The 'well-managed Boarding School for Young Ladies' has long closed; the soldiers have come and gone over the last two centuries, as the military needs of the country required them to be encamped within close distance of the coast and the port of Southampton.

The main waterway of the River Test runs to the west of the town, flowing from the chalk hills in the north of Hampshire to join Southampton water at Redbridge, but there are many diversions running through the town in a network of streams. As the 18th-century traveller commented, running water has been essential to the life of the town — it supplied power to the machinery of the corn, wool, papermaking and flax mills. The tanners and brewers needed ample water supplies, and the streams running through the townspeople's properties also provided a simple though not very salubrious solution to waste water problems.

The waterways flow around a core of firm dry land, an 'island' on which the earliest settlers lived amongst streams and marshland. The '-ey' ending to the name of Romsey possibly derives from the Old English word meaning island. (The meaning of the first part of the name is uncertain).

The pictures in this book show Romsey as a market town of a later

period; many of them were taken at the time when photography became very popular, and every building and important event was printed on a postcard.

The view from Greenhill on the west side of Romsey (49326) has not changed dramatically. In 1903 the Abbey, as now, dominated the town from this side, as it must have done when it was built in Norman times. But a hundred years ago the fields in the foreground were extensively farmed, with a strip of plots on the near side of the

river and water meadows on the far side. The Board Mill chimney and its buildings lay to the left of the mill owner's house, Rivermead. Sadler's Mill, on the extreme right of the picture, was, in 1903, an operating corn mill.

The pathway up Greenhill and another along the bottom to Squab Wood were favourite Sunday walks for Romsonians before the advent of the car.

In 1932 the new sewage treatment plant had been erected in the low building beyond the line of washing that we can see in 85037 (p12). Until this time the various streams of the River Test flowing through the town had provided a rudimentary drainage system for the properties on waterways. Those away from the streams had depended on the worthy efforts of the 'night soil' collectors and their horse-drawn load of buckets, which were taken to the 'sanitary fields'. Today there is a pumping station on the site — the main plant is now away to the left of picture 85037 (p12).

ROMSEY & THE RIVER TEST

he key to Romsey's early success as a settlement lies in the waters of the River Test, which approaches Romsey at Greatbridge. It leaves the town as it flows under Middlebridge to the south and enters Broadlands Park, once the farmlands of Romsey Abbey but a private estate since Tudor times. Amongst its owners have been Lord Palmerston, the Victorian prime minister, and Earl Mountbatten of Burma.

The main river still forms the beautiful western boundary to the town as it has done for hundreds of years. In the early 19th century, angling became a fashionable occupation for country gentlemen and their guests; the River Test was, and continued to be for many years, an ideal river for salmon and trout fishing. Now trout are commercially farmed in various places on the river.

The River Test and its various braids run alongside and through the town on its way to the sea. Up-river to the north of the town at Greatbridge, the Test divides into three channels. The Fishlake flows through the town centre; the main river passes under Greatbridge, and so does the channel supplying Greatbridge Mill, which milled corn for the Romsey area for several hundred years. The water supplying the power for this mill returns to the main river further downstream.

MIDDLEBRIDGE

With water in abundance, Romsey needed many bridges. The most important is Middlebridge, the main east-west crossing. In photograph 85042, we are looking south from Sadlers Mill towards the newly-built bridge to join the newly-constructed bypass.

With increasing traffic, particularly cars and lorries, the old bridge, built in 1781, was too narrow and steep. In its day the old bridge had been built on a wider scale than its three-arched predecessor. This was in response to the needs of the new turnpike roads that were using the crossing at this point. That work had involved the demolition of a house built on the south-east corner of the bridge, on the far left of 85042. The house just visible on the right was one of Romsey's many pubs, the Bridge Tavern, which closed in 1911.

The date of the first bridge here is unknown, but when the County Quarter Sessions was held in April 1608, it was reported that 'there is a great bridge of stone called Middle Bridge near the town of Romsey having long time been in great decay'. This bridge was used, according to the report, for 'the King's carriages to travel to

the New Forest and for his subjects to go to New Sarum and other towns in the West Country and to the town of Southampton from the West Country'.

It was decided at this court that if it was not repaired quickly, the costs would increase. It was ordered that the whole county

should share the cost, and that the inhabitants of Romsey were to contribute 'extraordinarily'. Romsey's inhabitants did not accept the order easily, insisting that the eastern bank of the river was the town boundary and that the bridge was not their responsibility. However, a compromise was arranged and the town paid part of the cost.

Although Greatbridge was destroyed during the Civil War, Middlebridge remained intact, but it was the scene of a skirmish between the Royalists and Parliamentarians. It continues to be the introduction to Romsey for travellers from the west, as it has been for centuries.

GREATBRIDGE 1903 49344

The buildings in this picture are cottages attached to Greatbridge Mill. About eight years after this picture was taken the bridge was rebuilt — it was a much more substantial structure to take the increased and heavier traffic. This was one of several rebuildings. At the time of the Civil War in the 17th century the bridge was considered to be of strategic importance, and was destroyed completely by Colonel Norton and his Parliamentary troops.

STANDING ON MIDDLEBRIDGE

SADLER'S MILL 1903 49342

THE RIVER, LOOKING NORTH FROM MIDDLEBRIDGE
C1955 R53028

The path beside the river is known as the Causeway. The main
way out of Romsey to the north of the town also shares this
name, indicating the need to watch the level of the river and
its propensity to flood. The Causeway, on the left, leads from
Middlebridge. It takes us to Sadler's Mill; from here there is a
footbridge to the park and the town centre.

To the north of Middlebridge is Sadler's Mill, the only
one of Romsey's nine mill-sites which worked on the
main river. There has been a mill on this site for many
hundreds of years.

The name Sadler's may relate to an owner of nearby property in
the 17th century; for much of the 19th and 20th centuries, it was
known as Burt's Mill, and through these centuries it operated as
a corn mill. The present building was constructed in the mid
18th century by the owner of Broadlands, Lord Palmerston. It ceased
to operate in 1968, and the main mill now stands empty and is being
renovated.

With nine mill sites in the town, many enterprises used water to
power the machinery necessary for their businesses — corn, paper,
and cloth-fulling mills, saw mills, and tanneries. Most written material
about Romsey's mills seems to relate to problems in obtaining that
most important item — water. Romsey's mills depended on the
river Test and its branches for their power. Competition was keen,
and resulted in many legal disputes arising from millers upstream
diverting the water from those downstream.

There was a series of disputes in Tudor times at Sadler's Mill: its
owner suffered from the work of millers upstream, who

'with divers and sondrie lewde and desperate persons ... erected a
pilinge over athwart the mayne Channel of the Ryver and thereby
stopped turned and diverted the said Mayne River of Terste out of
his aunciente and common Course ...'

Troubles of this kind continued through the following centuries,
providing the legal profession with a steady source of income. As
late as the early 20th century, wooden stakes were still being placed
incorrectly to control the water flow. At that time, photographic
evidence was offered in court; an unfortunate river keeper was shown
standing in the faulty area to demonstrate the depths.

STANDING ON MIDDLEBRIDGE

REAR OF SADLER'S MILL c1955 R53026

STANDING ON MIDDLEBRIDGE

THE RIVER TEST AND ITS COMMERCIAL USES

Photograph 51440, looking north-east, shows the minor streams which run round the Memorial Park to join the main flow. The point is near the end of the network of streams that break away from the main river north of the town.

In the past, these streams have been diverted and used commercially and domestically. Some of the new industries in Victorian and Edwardian times were less dependent on the River Test and its various braids, but Strong's brewery discharged effluents into the streams flowing through the site, and the Berthon Boat Works required water. This brainchild of the Rev E L Berthon, the vicar for the most of the last three decades of the 19th century, was first established close to the Vicarage, so that the water which bounded

his property could be used to test his new collapsible lifeboats.

The Boat Works grew into a very successful company, employing many skilled Romsonians. Although the original project was the building of collapsible lifeboats, the company enlarged its production, still on the 'collapsible' principle, to include boats of all sizes for a variety of purposes, pontoon bridges for use by armies both British and German, and even a collapsible bandstand. The works moved to a larger site in Portersbridge Street, now the Lortemore car park, and remained there until 1920, when it was sold and moved to Lymington, where the Berthon Boat Co still flourishes.

During the 19th century a succession of mill owners diversified from paper to various items, including patent leather for fashionable

THE RIVER TEST 1904 51440

THE RIVER TEST 1903 49343x

Just visible in the trees is the chimney of the mill known in 1903 as Abbey Mill 2 and later as Romsey Board Mills. This was one of many mills mentioned by the 18th-century traveller. In the 18th and early 19th centuries it produced writing paper — there are still Romsey documents in existence showing the watermark of this company.

shoes made from paper pulp. Later they turned their attention to 'Leather Boards, Glazed Press Paper, Jacquard and Dobie Card'. The Jacquard and Dobie Cards were punched cards used to control patterns on cloth looms.

The mill continued to make fibre board until its closure in 1967. The material used in the latter years was waste paper and cardboard — and sometimes shredded bank notes, brought in sacks and always accompanied by bank officials to see them pulped.

Houses were then built on the site of the mill's works, but this was not a typical 'brown field site' in modern planning terminology. The removal of the mill buildings opened up the area to the beauty of the river and the views of Green Hill and Squab Wood.

INTO THE TOWN CENTRE

The town is almost equidistant from Winchester, Southampton, and Salisbury — and the population grew but very little during the 19th century, when those other cities were expanding. Earlier, Romsey had grown more successfully as a result of the coaching trade. The building of the toll roads in the mid 18th century had brought business to Romsey's inns. The roads from Salisbury to Southampton and from Winchester to the west crossed the river here. Mainstone, on the west side of the bridge, and Middlebridge Street on the east side, provided the necessary refreshment stops for local traffic.

The group of houses on the west side of Middlebridge, on the main road to Ringwood and Lyndhurst and Salisbury, is known as Mainstone. This very small settlement was well provided with 'watering-holes'. Just to the right in picture 51442, immediately over the bridge, was the Bridge Tavern, now a private house. In the middle was the Lamb Inn, where William Young kept a lodging house. A few steps on was the Horse and Jockey, conveniently placed on the turning into the Salisbury road. These were just a few of the 40 or so public houses in Romsey at the time.

There were another three public houses in Middlebridge Street, which leads to Bell Street and the southern entry to the Market Place. Both streets had their own establishments. Although it should be remembered that water was not always safe to drink, Romsey did have a reputation for alcoholic over-indulgence — there is a local saying, 'so drunk he must have been to Romsey'.

Middlebridge Street, on the town side of the bridge from Mainstone, had tanneries and saw mills as well as bakeries and butchers' shops, all employing labourers who needed to quench their thirst, as did travellers to the town.

Strong's Brewery was the name with which Romsey was closely associated until some 30 years ago. 'You are now in the Strong Country' was the well-known advertising sign which you could see when travelling through Hampshire by road or rail.

MAINSTONE 1904
51442

This famous firm was developed from a combination of various Romsey breweries in the latter part of the 19th century, when rail transport made it possible to carry beer over considerable distances. Strong's became one of the main employers in the town for about a hundred years, but the need for modernisation caused brewing to cease in 1981; the operation, by that time part of Whitbread Wessex, was finally closed in 1990. Part of the site has been cleared, but the main buildings, some converted to offices, remain — the heritage of late 19th-century and early 20th-century builders.

INTO THE TOWN CENTRE

BELL STREET

Romsey lies on the main communication roads between Salisbury and Southampton and between Winchester and Ringwood (and the west country). Before the bypass was built in 1931 all traffic passed through the Market Place, and that travelling to or from the west travelled up and down Bell Street, now a one-way street (see R53031).

In earlier times, the most important building in the street was the Town Mill, now the site of the Duke's Mill shopping precinct. The water for the Town Mill came from another off-shoot stream of the River Test. It runs at the back of the properties on the eastern side of Bell Street, and is still visible from the bus station. On the western side of the street, yet another stream Runs at the back of the properties, but this is now underground.

With the improved turnpike roads of the 18th and 19th century the Bell Inn, the building on the right of picture R53031, became one of the town's important coaching inns, with stabling for 18 horses. Its importance changed the name of the street, which had been known until then as Mill Street. However, the first railway arrived in Romsey in the 1840s and dealt a death blow to the coaching trade. The Bell survived for two decades and then closed in the 1860s with the opening of a second railway line. The building became the business premises of the Roles family, architects and builders, and has now been converted into offices. One of the family, William Comely Roles, worked for Sir Edwin Lutyens, the famous architect, before designing and building houses on his own account. Mr Roles' work in Romsey includes the United Reformed Church manse and the Bartlett's almshouses in Abbey Meads. Bartlett's almshouses were originally built in the early part of the 19th century at the end of Middlebridge Street, close to the bridge. They were demolished and relocated in Abbey Meads to make room for the bypass in the early 1930s.

At the beginning of the 20th century there were three other public houses in Bell Street: the Angel, which is now a restaurant called La Parisienne; the Cross Keys, which closed as a public house in 1972; and the Queen's Head or Royal Oak, which closed in 1911. Until the latter part of the 19th century, Romsey's shops were mostly small one-room

BELL STREET c1955 R53031

MARKET PLACE 1904 51431

businesses, with the owner living above the shop, and possibly a workshop at the back. There were numerous butchers, bakers, dairies, tobacconists, sweetshops and corner shops selling a variety of useful articles.

The shops in Bell Street were not all small. Towards the end of the 19th century, Mr Tom Summers was the proprietor of a large draper's shop. (Part of Bradbeer's department store is on the same site.) In 1881 he employed seven assistants, of whom three were young ladies who lived on the premises and three were his own sons. Next door, his father Mr Charles Summers ran an outfitters' shop supplying gentlemen's clothing. The other large 'emporium', Guards, in Church Street sold both ladies' and men's clothing and employed living-in staff to make some of the garments. When the telephone arrived, Mr Guard insisted on 'Romsey 1' as his number.

A few doors down from the Summers' shops is the Baptist Church, built in 1811 and well supported from its early days by the shopkeepers and tradesmen of the town.

THE BUILDINGS OF THE MARKET PLACE

The central statue in the Market Place is of the third Lord Palmerston, Victorian prime minister and owner of nearby Broadlands, who died in 1865. The statue was erected in 1868. A great national figure, he nevertheless showed a keen interest in the town's affairs, writing in his own hand to the mayor on very basic matters; for instance, he suggested that the Corporation should take steps to improve sanitation in the town if they were to avoid outbreaks of typhoid. The suggestion was given much serious consideration before some essential action was eventually taken some thirty years later.

The building on the left of photograph 51431 is the Post and Telegraph Office. Its upper curved wall is faced with mathematical tiles, which are contrived to look like bricks. It is separated by the entrance to Bell Street from the Town Hall and the two businesses of Henry Harding, who ran one as a fishmonger and poulterer and the other as a fruiterer and grocer.

The Town Hall, an imposing Victorian structure, replaced a much smaller building with charming Dutch gables. It is Romsey's fourth civic building and close to the site of the second one, the Audit

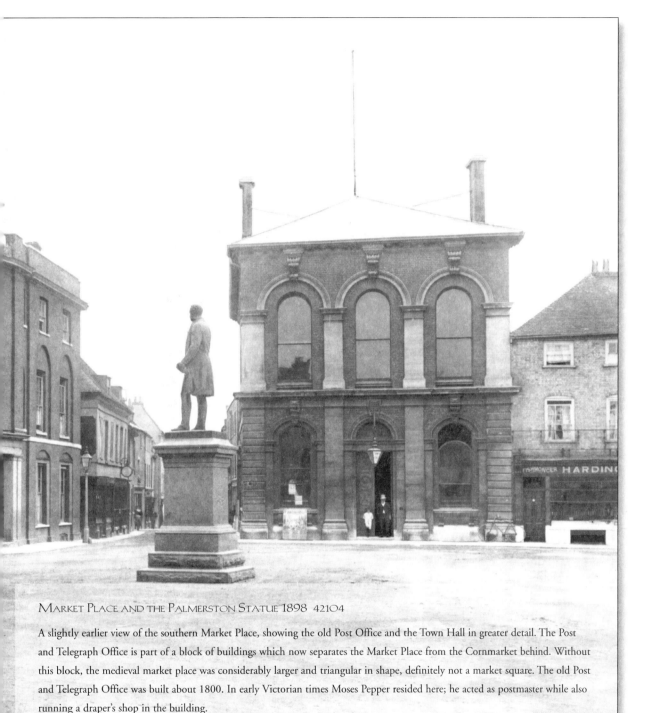

MARKET PLACE AND THE PALMERSTON STATUE 1898 42104

A slightly earlier view of the southern Market Place, showing the old Post Office and the Town Hall in greater detail. The Post and Telegraph Office is part of a block of buildings which now separates the Market Place from the Cornmarket behind. Without this block, the medieval market place was considerably larger and triangular in shape, definitely not a market square. The old Post and Telegraph Office was built about 1800. In early Victorian times Moses Pepper resided here; he acted as postmaster while also running a draper's shop in the building.

INTO THE TOWN CENTRE

Above:
MARKET PLACE,
THE WHITE HORSE HOTEL
1903 49336

Left:
THE WHITE HORSE HOTEL
1903 49340

House, which had become decrepit by 1820. To take its place, the Corporation bought and developed a redundant malthouse near the west end of the Abbey. This building served as Town Hall and Town Jail for some 40 years. Then it was felt that Romsey needed to keep up with the spirit of the times, and in 1866 the Market Place was dominated by the new edifice.

It must have gladdened the hearts of the modernists. For the next hundred years it remained the home of Romsey Borough Council until the reorganisation of local government in 1974. This caused the building to become the property of the newly created Test Valley Borough Council, and in order to retain it for the town's own Mayor and Town Council, the townsfolk had to buy it back. This was done, and the building was totally renovated. It is now used for public meetings and functions as well as for civic purposes.

The White Horse has been an important inn in Romsey market place for many centuries despite the rather dull Georgian façade it had at the time of photograph 49336A (it looked brighter later in the 20th century). The present building, largely timber-framed, dates from Tudor times and has Tudor wall paintings, but there is evidence in the cellars of an even earlier building. It has always been used by the local inhabitants as well as travellers. This was particularly so in the case of property auctioneers and the market fraternity in the 19th century.

In 1838, the Hampshire Advertiser reported: 'Romsey Cattle Market — Good Christmas exhibition of stock at this rising market. The show is the best since the establishment of the market and attendance greater. At 2 o'clock supporters and friends sat down to dinner at the White Horse. The fare was bountiful, substantial and well served. The liquors were good enough to induce many, even of the staid and steady class, to indulge in 'one bottle more'.

THE CONSERVATIVE CLUB 1903 49337

Sir John Barker Mill in the Chair kept up the merriment and harmony into the evening'.

Dr John Latham, writing about Romsey in 1820, said: 'This town is on a leading road to the west and a good thoroughfare with good inns viz the White Horse which is the principal one. The public is accommodated with post chaises and horses, besides which stage coaches pass daily to London, Portsmouth, Southampton, Salisbury and from the latter to Bath, Bristol and many other places westward'.

In the prime of the coaching trade, the mid 18th century, the White Horse had thirty-five beds, six rooms and stabling for fifty horses and room for four carriages. Although the much-enlarged modern hotel has thirty-three bedrooms now, thirty-five beds did not mean thirty-five bedrooms three hundred years ago. There were probably one or two dormitory-style rooms, and staff slept over the stables or where they worked.

Behind the photographer of 49340 (p33) were the livery stables, now converted to hotel accommodation. At that time the stables were the home of the horse that pulled the trap carrying customers to and from the railway station, and that also pulled the fire engine when the fire service was called to an emergency.

There had been a public house for many centuries on the north-west corner of the Market Place (see 49337). It was known as the Swan, and a renovation some thirty years ago revealed wattle and daub walls. It was one of the important hostelries of the town in Victorian times, and was used for activities such as the supper in 1880 for sixty men who worked for Mr Wheeler, builder, and Mr Marshall, house decorator. In 1873 the Romsey & South Hampshire Chronicle reported on the cattle market in the Swan Hotel yard for 'Bullocks, Heifers, Cows, Sheep, Lambs, and Horses'. Presumably the sale ring was held in the hotel yard whilst the animals were penned in the Market Place.

Towards the end of the 19th century, the inn was bought by David Faber, the businessman behind the fast-growing Strong's Brewery. He then sold it to the newly-formed Romsey Conservative Workingmen's Club. For some time the corner ground floor and cellar were separately tenanted. There are many legends in the town's folk history of underground

passages from the Abbey out into the town, and the cellars of the Club form part of these stories. Unfortunately, there is a deep flowing stream under the buildings on the west side of Church Street and the Market Place, separating them from the Abbey property, so the stories seem a little difficult to substantiate.

The streets converging on the Market Place are all narrow, but they have been widened in the past. There were traffic problems then as now. Church Street, the route to the north of the town, was until about 1880 about 16ft in width including the pavements — it was very difficult for carriages or wagons to pass.

MARKET PLACE C1955 R53017

Above:
MARKET PLACE C1965 R53062A

The old inn sign is now attached to the Conservative Club building, but it was moved there from the Bell Inn when that hostelry in Bell Street closed. During the Civil War two centuries earlier, two of Cromwell's soldiers are reputed to have been hanged from the Swan's inn sign, but not from the particular bracket on the wall today.

INTO THE TOWN CENTRE

The Market Place has been the hub of the town since medieval times. The Abbess of Romsey Abbey was granted the right to hold markets by Royal Charter in the early 12th century. Market day has varied through the centuries; under the Abbess it was held on Sundays. Later, in the 17th century, market day changed to Saturday, and in Victorian times it was held on Thursdays. Then in 1919 the market was moved to a new site off Bell Street.

During the last 150 years the exteriors of the upper floors of the buildings in the Market Place have changed little. The shop fronts have been modernised and the trades have changed, but the upper stories remain much the same. In 1903 many of the owners of the shops lived on the premises, and even today some of the upper storeys are still residential.

In 1903 the Georgian house (see 49335) with the Abbey tower rising behind was a private house. By 1932 (see 85041) it had become a bank, but the only exterior alteration was the replacing of the doorway to the extreme left. Waters the stationers and lending library, with its windows lit by large gas lamps, has been replaced by the modern equivalent —W H Smith Ltd. Instead of butchers' and fresh fish shops in the Market Place, there are travel agents, estate agents, and opticians, but there is still a pharmacy in the place where there has been one for at least a hundred years.

By the middle of the 20th century some small towns were suffering from the desire to modernise, and they lost many of their older buildings. Fortunately, Romsey has never rushed to keep up with the latest trends. Although national chain shops arrived, as did the motor car, the buildings survived; only the style of their occupancy changed.

Above:
MARKET PLACE 1903 49335

Right:
MARKET PLACE 1932 85041

To the left in the south-west corner of the Market Place, is the gateway into the site of the old monastic precinct. The road within is called The Abbey.

Left:
ABBEY HOUSE CONVENT 1932 85044

Below:
ABBEY WALK 1904 51439

FROM THE MARKET PLACE TOWARDS THE ABBEY

Abbey House Convent (see 85044) is at the end of a long drive off the road called The Abbey. In 1891 the Bishop of Portsmouth, at the request of Hampshire County Council, established an orphanage for Roman Catholic boys using the existing house, then known as Abbey House, and adding other buildings to the site. The house is close to the Abbey, and was originally part of the Abbey property. Apparently it was not possible to find English nuns to staff the orphanage, and the work was undertaken by the Sisters of La Sagesse, a French order of nuns. It was some time before these ladies from Brittany, dressed in their long skirts, cloaks and very large head coverings, were accepted in the town.

By the 1930s child care policy had changed, and the orphans went to live in smaller homes. The nuns then opened a fee-paying school for girls, both day girls and boarders, and a pre-preparatory school for boys. It continued until almost the end of the 20th century as La Sagesse Convent School, but it has now closed. The site is being developed for private housing and a nursing home; the nuns still reside in the old Abbey House.

The building to the right of 85044 is the Roman Catholic Church, built in the style of the Arts and Crafts Movement. This was the first

Into the Town Centre

Above:
THE WAR MEMORIAL PARK 1932 85043

Left:
THE WAR MEMORIAL PARK C1955 R53021

Catholic church to be built in Romsey since the nuns left the Abbey when King Henry VIII closed the monasteries and convents, but it has no connection with the medieval Benedictine nunnery.

In close proximity is the United Reformed Church, which stands near to the site of the first Dissenting Chapel; not far away in Bell Street is the Baptist Church. In the later 1700s the Quakers had a meeting house nearby. The first Methodist Church was close to Bell Street, but the present building is a little further away from this 'ecumenical' area.

The road called The Abbey bears right around the west end of Romsey Abbey. The way ahead, once known as Abbey Walk, is now The Meads (see 51439, p41); it leads to the Memorial Park and then, by a footpath, to the river at Sadler's Mill. The whole way from the Abbey gateway to the park area was very busy in the past. In the early 19th century the Latham brewery was adjacent to the Abbey, around the turning to the right of picture 51439, while the road led to the paper mill, which continued to operate until the 1960s. The brick entrance on the left of the picture is the gateway to the Abbey House Convent.

The Memorial Park (see 85043 and R53021) was established after the First World War to be a fitting place for the erection of the memorial to honour the dead of that war. Later the bandstand was built, and the town band and other visiting bands gave concerts on summer afternoons and evenings. It is very near the river, and a rather wet area. In order to make it suitable for a town park, hard core was laid from the wartime Remount Camp which had been established on Pauncefoot Hill a mile or so away. This camp was opened in November 1914 and closed in 1919; it was a very large centre for the training and rehabilitation of horses and other animals used for transport during the First World War.

After the Second World War more names were added to the memorial, which have been joined since then by names from subsequent conflicts. The bandstand was replaced by a Japanese gun presented to the town by Earl Mountbatten. In 2000 the gun was removed for repair to its main structure for it had been exposed to the weather and used as a children's climbing frame for over fifty years. A new and elegant bandstand was erected and the renovated gun placed in a different position, but still used as a climbing frame. The park now boasts tennis courts, a bowling green, a children's play area, and a refreshment kiosk.

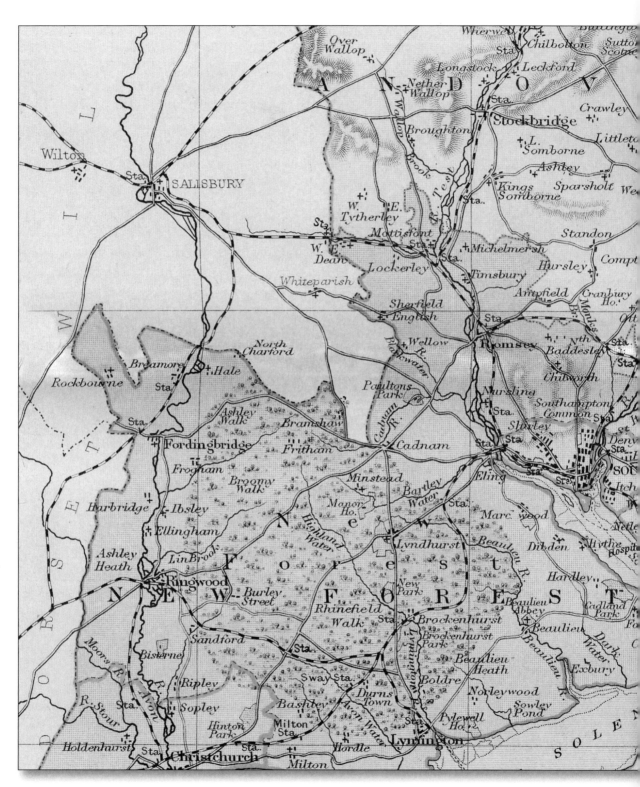

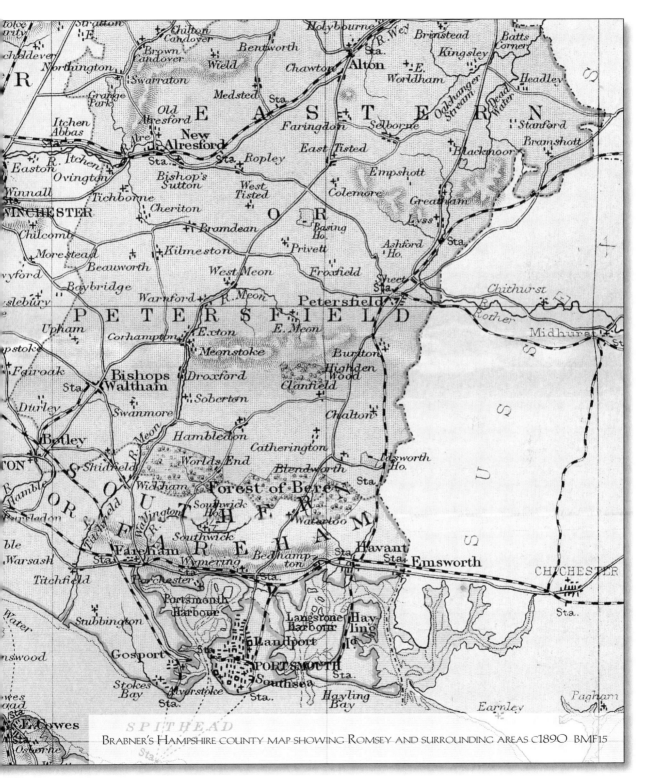

Brabner's Hampshire county map showing Romsey and surrounding areas c1890 BMF15

THE ABBEY AND ITS SURROUNDINGS

THE ABBEY AND ITS SURROUNDINGS

Above: THE ABBEY 1898 42096

Returning from the Memorial Park it was once possible to enjoy the view of Romsey Abbey we see in 42096, but it is now obscured by housing. The meadow, used on occasions as a pleasure ground for festivities by the townspeople, is now part of the 20th-century residential development to the west of the Abbey and the Market Place.

In medieval times, when the Abbey was a nunnery, its domestic buildings were on the south side of the church. Traces of the monastic structures can be seen inside some of the houses now on that site. The building immediately adjacent to the Abbey, and partly hidden by a tree in 42096, was part of the brewery owned by John Latham. It later served as the Town Hall, with jail attached, and was then replaced by the present Church Rooms.

The striking triple lancet windows on the west side of the Abbey (see 63770, p48) show the height of the nave, which rises to some 80ft. There is no west door, since the townspeople entered from the north, and the nuns from the south, where they had their extensive domestic buildings.

Romsey Abbey is said to be the only Norman nunnery church still standing in England. After being in existence for six hundred years, the nunnery was closed in 1539. By then only a few nuns remained, and the Crown took the nunnery's possessions. The church was spared, since the people of Romsey were using it as their parish church and were able to raise the huge sum of £100 demanded by King Henry VIII for this most important Romsey building.

The vicarage (see 85045, p50) was erected in the middle of the 19th century very close to the Abbey. Until then, the vicars of Romsey had to provide their own accommodation. The stone of which it is built and the windows blend well with its surroundings. The Vicarage had a large garden behind it extending down to the river. Unfortunately, this elegant Victorian building became unsuitable for modern 20th-century vicars; it was sold and replaced by a smaller, more comfortable building close by. The old Vicarage is now a private house called Folly House, named after the reconstructed Abbey features in the garden.

The Church School, which we can see in photograph 85046A (p51), was built in 1851 as the National School for Girls and Infants; it included accommodation for the headmistress. As the stone in the wall records, 'these Schools were erected as his last gift to the Parishioners of Romsey by the Hon and Rev Gerard T Noel,

THE ABBEY AND ITS SURROUNDINGS

The Abbey 1911 63770

The Abbey and its Surroundings

THE VICARAGE 1932 85045

Vicar Feb 8 AD 1851'. The Gothic style of architecture used for the building blends well with the great Abbey nearby. There are modern extensions at the back and a large playing field, but the school still retains its original appearance. As Romsey Abbey Primary School, it continues to be a Church School.

This girls' and infants' school and the boys' school were supported by the Church of England. The boys' school was originally held in the Abbey; then later it had its home in Middlebridge Street, and afterwards in Station Road. Both Sunday and day schools had been run by churches of all denominations from early in the 19th century in a variety of buildings, and by the middle of the 19th century the Nonconformist churches were supporting a new purpose-built school for boys, girls and infants on the other side of the town.

The varied shapes of the windows on the north side of the Abbey (see 42101, p52) are the result of extensions and demolitions in the past. While the Abbey was a Benedictine nunnery, the townspeople worshipped in the north aisle; this became too small, and was extended northwards in the 15th century. When the nuns left and the whole building became the parish church, this extension was demolished. Its windows were used to plug the open archways that had been made during the earlier extension. Part of the demolished stonework was many years later re-erected in the garden of the vicarage. To the left of the transept, along the lower roof line, there are some interesting and amusing carved

CHURCH OF ENGLAND SCHOOL, CHURCH LANE
1932 85046

THE ABBEY AND ITS SURROUNDINGS

corbels. The graveyard on the north side of the Abbey was used for centuries by the townspeople. In 1857 burials here ceased, and a cemetery was opened in Botley Road.

The appearance of the Abbey's north side was changed in 1907 with the erection of a porch over the door, which we can see in photograph R53037 (p54). This was built using funds raised when a great festival and pageant were held to celebrate what was thought to be the thousandth anniversary of the arrival of the first nuns. The Millenary Pageant was a national event, written and produced by a professional, and attended by the Archbishop of Canterbury and other distinguished visitors, some of whom came by the special trains laid on by the London and South Western Railway. The cross in the graveyard, which is known as the North Garth, was erected at the same time. The gravestones were later removed, and some were laid around the cross.

Now the Parish Church, the Abbey was built during the 12th and early 13th centuries. The stone came from the Isle of Wight and Wiltshire, an immense undertaking considering the difficulties of transport and the enormous quantities required. The sturdy Norman building has a squat tower with a wooden structure on top which has been described as 'an octagonal wooden hen coop'. This is the belfry, in which hangs a fine peal of eight bells.

There was once a spacious chapel extending beyond the present east wall we see in picture 49328 (p56). The 14th-century windows with their characteristic pointed arches came from the chapel, which was severely truncated in the 16th century. The church is uniquely dedicated to St Mary and St Ethelflæda.

The south-east view of the Abbey (42098, p56) shows its cruciform shape. The eastern end was the earliest part of the present Norman church, which was built over a Saxon one. The first known Abbess was a granddaughter of King Alfred the Great. From the time of its foundation, the Abbey drew well-born ladies as nuns, and daughters and sons of important families were sent here to be educated. Queen Margaret of Scotland's daughters came here to be in the care of their aunt, Christina, who was one of the nuns. The elder princess married King Henry I in 1100, and became known as 'Good Queen Maud'.

The ladders on the roof which we can see in photograph 42098 (p56) are a reminder of the constant care necessary to

The Abbey, North Side 1898 42101

The Abbey and its Surroundings

maintain such an ancient building. The private garden with the large greenhouse belonged to a house whose front entrance was in the Market Place. The garden area has since been restored to Abbey ownership.

The wealth and importance of the Abbey is shown by its great length of 263 feet and its proportionate width. In the 14th century there were about a hundred nuns, most of whom would have brought dowries. Timber, land and estates were granted to the Abbey, and a steward was employed to manage its properties, which were scattered over Hampshire and beyond. As well as the nuns and the children being educated here, there were many servants.

The Abbess, who was chosen by the nuns, held a very important position. She was not only the spiritual leader: she had secular responsibilities too, both in the town and relating to the Abbey's wealthy properties in other parts of the country. The Black Death in 1349, which decimated the whole population of the country, badly affected the Abbey. Many nuns died, and their numbers never exceeded twenty-five in later years.

THE ABBEY, NORTH FRONT C1960 R53037

THE ABBEY AND ITS SURROUNDINGS

Above:
THE ABBEY 1903 49328

Right:
THE ABBEY, FROM THE SOUTH-EAST 1898
42098

THE ABBEY CRUCIFIX 1898 42102

The Abbey's beautiful 11th-century rood, or crucifix, is on the west side of the south transept. Jesus is shown with head held high, arms firmly outstretched and feet not crossed. Above his head, coming down from a cloud, is the hand of God. The sculpture portrays a triumphant figure of a living Christ who rules from the Cross. The rectangular recess on the right may have been used for a lamp or to burn incense when this wall was within the monastic cloisters, before the destruction that followed the Dissolution in 1539.

THE NORMAN DOOR 1899 42976

The Abbess's Doorway has a variety of late Norman decoration. The nuns' living apartments were on this south side of the church, and the corbel stones that used to support the cloister roof still remain. The sloping scar we can see in the photograph shows where an outhouse was built after the door was blocked up. Fortunately, this served to protect the finely-carved ancient crucifix for many years.

INSIDE THE ABBEY

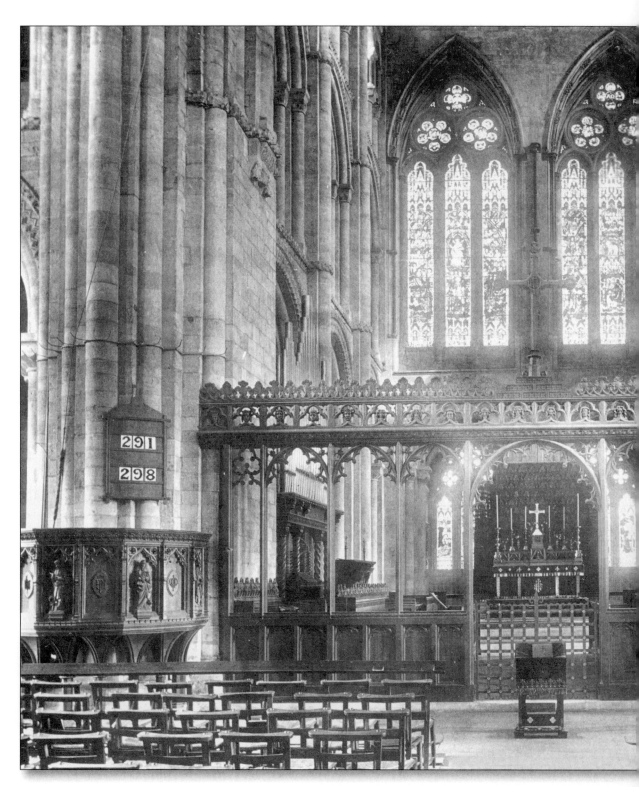

As we look towards the east end of the Abbey (42977A), we see the Victorian glass in the windows, which is dedicated to Lord Mount Temple of Broadlands. The high altar is beneath these windows, but the Abbey also has several other altars in the chapels, which are used regularly. The wooden pulpit is also Victorian; it is carved with figures of the Evangelists. The nave once held pews where there are now chairs. On the right of the aisle was the large Broadlands pew, which had heavy curtains round it to keep out the draughts.

The view from the west end of the nave (51433, p60) shows the change in the architectural style of the arches. Those at the eastern end follow the plain early Norman fashion, whilst those on the western end, seen at either side in the foreground of 51433, are the pointed arches of the Early English style. The change arose because the western end of the nave was completed some 130 years after building began.

On the wall below the far window at the west end of the nave (see 42979, p61) are memorials to the Palmerston family — one is by Flaxman. The original Deed of Sale of the Abbey to the town, with Henry VIII's signature, is on display in the small treasury in the south aisle.

THE ABBEY,
THE SCREEN AND THE CHOIR 1899 42977A

INSIDE THE ABBEY

Above:
THE ABBEY, NAVE EAST 1904 51433

Left:
THE GURNEY STOVES 1904 51433A

The Gurney coke-burning stoves were introduced by the Vicar, with financial support from Lord Palmerston, in the 1860s to provide some heat in the church; they were used for a hundred years.

Above: THE TAYLOR MEMORIAL 1932 85060

Near the north door of the Abbey is a lifelike figure of a sleeping child clasping a rosebud in her hand. It is the effigy of the young daughter of a Romsey surgeon, Dr Francis Taylor, who was also a skilled sculptor. He carved this memorial to his little girl, who had died of scarlet fever after a short illness. His artistry was widely acknowledged. A figure of Christ bearing the Cross, sculpted by him, was accepted for display in London at the Great Exhibition of 1851. This effigy of the child was first placed over her grave in the North Garth.

Below: THE ABBEY, THE SCREEN AND THE CHOIR 1899 42979

EASTWARDS FROM THE MARKET PLACE

From the far east end of the Market Place, the Abbey still dominates the view (42105A). The Corn Exchange, built in 1864, was originally planned to be associated with the new Town Hall. The parties involved in the project were unable to agree, and two new buildings graced the centre of the town in the same decade.

Corn trading tends to be a seasonal occupation, and the building had many other uses. The cellars were kept as a bonded warehouse by Strong's and earlier by George's, both Romsey brewers. The local Volunteer Brigade of the Hampshire Regiment used it as a Drill Hall, Headquarters and Armoury, and during the both World Wars it was used as a recreation club for the military.

In 1924 the Corn Exchange Company went out of business, and the building changed hands. The large main hall was divided and an upper floor was inserted, which meant that the windows had to be changed, as we see in 85040 (p64). Barclays Bank and Hook Bros, grocers, were established on the ground floor. The second floor served various purposes, including a billiard hall, a cinema, and an auction mart.

In 1932 motor vehicles were beginning to fill the streets. There were no one-way systems or parking regulations, although the Town Council were aware of the growing problems. They were in discussion with the police about the desirability of all traffic turning left when coming into the Market Place. Earlier, in 1931, the parking problem in the Market Place was resolved by the Mayor writing to the owners of the cars causing difficulties — 'and the problem ceased'.

Although the bypass had just been built, buses and coaches still came through the centre of the town. Their main stop was the Market Place, and it would seem from the road signs that we can see in 85040 that visiting travellers needed to be told how to reach Bournemouth and Salisbury.

Until the early 19th century, the Market Place included the area now known as the Corn Market (see R53011, p66). In those earlier times, this part was called the Pig Market; there were many complaints about the butchers who left their chopping blocks and rubbish outside their shops. There are still two independent butchers trading in this part of Romsey.

Among the buildings on the southern side of the Corn Market, the Dolphin Hotel (R53012A, p66) has a Georgian frontage with a

Above:
THE CORN EXCHANGE 1898 42105

Left:
WATER TROUGH OUTSIDE THE CORN EXCHANGE 1903
49338 (DETAIL)

In 1886 the owner of Broadlands, the Rt Hon William Cowper-Temple, MP, presented the town with the water trough outside the Corn Exchange. It provided water at different levels for human beings, horses and dogs. In these more hygienic days it is filled with flowers in the summer months.

EASTWARDS FROM THE MARKET PLACE

THE OLD CORN EXCHANGE 1932 85040

EASTWARDS FROM THE MARKET PLACE

Above:
THE CORN MARKET c1955 R53011

Left:
THE CORN MARKET c1955 R53012A

The Tudor Rose is one of Romsey's oldest buildings. In Victorian times, its ancient history was forgotten, and it was known as the Bugle. It is thought to have been built in the 15th century, possibly for the formal use of one of the Romsey Guilds. Renovations in the 1920s disclosed its age. The removal of walls upstairs uncovered a half-timbered hall with a stone fireplace. As a result of these discoveries, the Bugle was given a new name more suitable to its age: the Tudor Rose.

Opposite:
MARKET PLACE c1955 R53007

EASTWARDS FROM THE MARKET PLACE

much older building at the rear. During the 18th century, it was one of the larger inns offering accommodation to coaching travellers. It has now been renovated and incorporated into the new Bradbeer's store and the sign of the Dolphin replaced by the sign of the 19th century store owner.

Leaving the Market Place and the Cornmarket and travelling east, the 18th-century traveller would have crossed a bridge over another of the River Test's streams (it is now underground at this point). He would then enter the street known as The Hundred. It is thought to take its name from the early land division of a shire or county, and this stream was one of the boundaries between two hundreds. Timothy Whites' shop stands at the entrance to The Hundred.

Timothy Whites' building, now Boots, is a typical example of a modern shop front added to an old building. The top floor remains the same as it was when the building was the shop and offices of an agricultural and horticultural seed merchants more than a hundred years ago. That had been another conversion from the original house,

which was probably built in the 18th century. Elcombes, the seed merchants, grew much of their own stock in land behind the shop and on a larger plot to the north of the town.

THE HUNDRED AND BEYOND

As we enter the Hundred, we are leaving the commercial part of the town: the Hundred becomes the road to Winchester, with a turning off to Southampton in the south. Photograph 63781 (p68) shows architecture of differing periods. The thatched roofs and the lath and plaster walls of the cottages are typical of working people's houses of the earlier centuries. The woman looking out of her door is next to a window built with a sideways sliding opening, dating from the days before pavements, when a casement would have projected into the road. In similar style, but with shutters, is the Sawyers Arms, one of the many public houses. They sold beer brewed at another alehouse not far away.

Further along the street, it is possible to see the apex of a flint building lying back from the road. This is Romsey Police Station;

EASTWARDS FROM THE MARKET PLACE

it looks today much as it did when it was built in Victorian times.

Further east, at the point shown in 63780, the street was still called the Hundred in 1911. Over the years since then it has been known as Winchester Street, and now, in the 21st century, it is called Winchester Road.

The house with the clock high on its wall, known as the Clock House, was built in 1862 as a replacement tollhouse for the turnpike road to Winchester. It was larger than most such houses and had a weighbridge outside in order to assess the correct tolls. It stood at the junction of the roads to Winchester and to Southampton. When the photograph was taken, it was the home of a lady who repaired umbrellas, and one was hung outside as a sign.

On the left is a terrace of Victorian houses clad in the popular Virginia creeper which turns red in autumn. The horse and wagon is outside the Crown, a substantially-built inn with a wide side entrance, which is said to date back to the days of the stage coach. The hanging sign showing a crown was made of copper.

These Victorian houses were part of the easterly growth of the town. At the end of the 19th and the beginning of the 20th century, the owners and managers of the larger shops and

Above:
THE HUNDRED 1911 63781

Left:
THE HUNDRED 1911 63780

EASTWARDS FROM THE MARKET PLACE

Fox Mill on the Bypass c1960 R53044

Fox Mill was one of Romsey's shorter-lived mills. The mill was built almost opposite the gates into Broadlands at the end of the 18th century, and it had closed by the end of the 19th century. It was the only mill to operate with water from the Tadburn stream, which flows into the Test near Middlebridge. The Tadburn stream only had sufficient water for the mill after taking waste water from the Andover to Redbridge Canal, which ran on the eastern side of the town. The Canal had a short life as a commercial operation, opening in 1794 and closing in 1859. The southern bypass of the town was built in the 1930s; its route was partly along an existing path which ran by the Tadburn stream to Fox Mill from the Southampton Road.

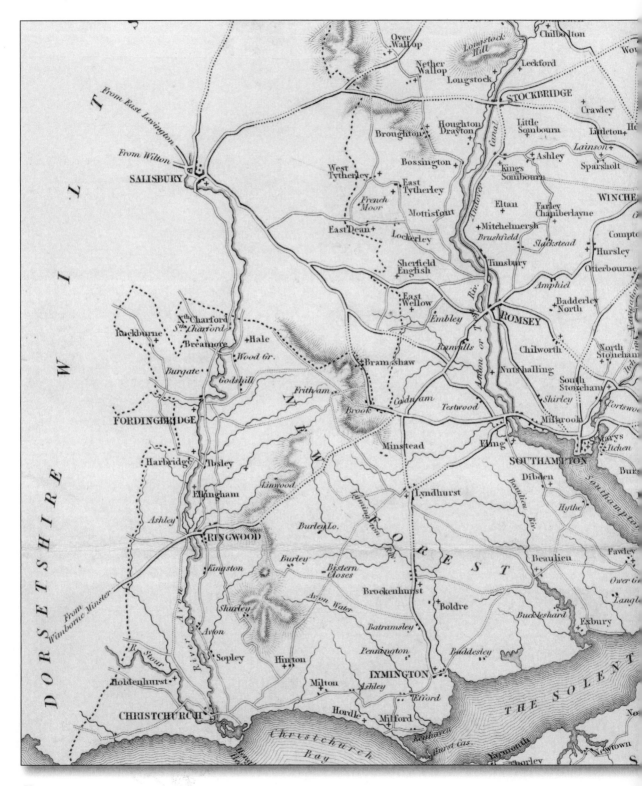

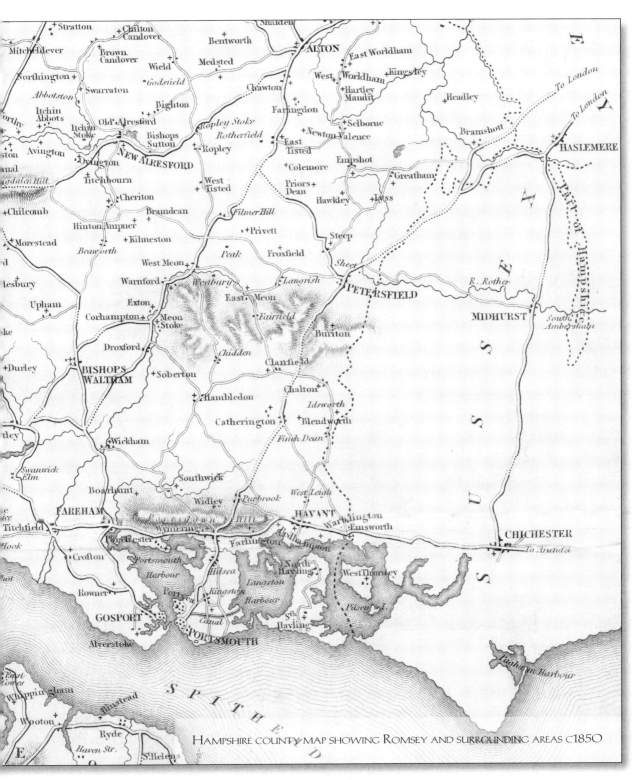

HAMPSHIRE COUNTY MAP SHOWING ROMSEY AND SURROUNDING AREAS c1850

OUT AND ABOUT - BROADLANDS & EMBLEY PARK

Broadlands stands on the southern side of the bypass and by the river Test. The estate was one of the properties of the Convent; it was sold when the nuns left the Abbey. The Georgian house we see today was built by the Palmerston family, whose most famous member was the Victorian statesman.

The first Viscount Palmerston bought the property in 1736 for £26,000 from the family who had owned it since its confiscation by Henry VIII from the Abbess. Since then it has never been sold again — the new owners have each passed it to their descendants, who live here today. The house is built on raised ground which gently slopes down to the river. Three miles of this clear chalk stream flow through the grounds on its way to Southampton Water.

After 1767 the old Jacobean house was rebuilt by the second Viscount Palmerston; he employed 'Capability' Brown not only to lay out the grounds, but also to design the mansion in the elegant classical style. It remains as one of the finest examples of Palladian architecture. The steps on the side we see in 42110 lead up to the saloon, which has delicately-gilded plaster decoration on the ceiling and walls. The building is finely furnished, but being smaller than many stately homes, it has a feeling of a comfortable family house. It is open to the public in the summer.

In 1939 the estate was inherited by Edwina Ashley, who married Lord Louis Mountbatten, and as Earl and Countess Mountbatten of Burma they made their home at Broadlands. It is now the residence of their grandson, Lord Romsey.

During the Second World War most of the house was used to replace part of the bombed Southampton Hospital. In 1954 the extension was demolished, and the house was restored to its original classical shape. The house has

Broadlands 1898 42110

BROADLANDS 1898 42111

The Victorian extension to the left was added as a workroom and billiard room for the third Viscount Palmerston. Behind is a wing built to accommodate the many guests who stayed at Broadlands.

Out and About - Broadlands & Embley Park

BROADLANDS 1904 51446

The south front of Broadlands has a central door; the carriage entrance is on the east side, with a portico which protects those arriving and departing. On the right is a heated orangery built in the classical style. On the left is one of the old cedar of Lebanon trees.

a centre of hospitality over the centuries. An early visitor was James I in 1607, when he planted two mulberry trees, which still survive. 350 years later, two more were planted by the Queen and Prince Philip, when their hosts were the Mountbattens. More than two hundred individual trees have been planted in the grounds here by famous people.

In earlier days famous actors, painters and writers, including Garrick, Sheridan and Reynolds, were guests. Later, in the time of Palmerston's heir, William Cowper-Temple, the new generation of authors and artists came, amongst whom were Ruskin and Dante Gabriel Rossetti. Rossetti arrived ill and depressed by the sudden

death of his wife. The peace he found here and the beautiful flowering magnolia trees growing on this side of the house inspired him to paint again.

From 1872, great religious conferences were held in the grounds annually. These brought together Christians of all denominations, and hundreds attended. The windows on the left (51446) are of the drawing room where the first meeting of the Church Army was held. Nowadays the annual Romsey Agricultural Show, bringing town and country together, is held in the grounds of Broadlands.

Embley Park lies off the road to Salisbury. Impressive gates lead through the well-kept grounds to the house. The central bay window

OUT AND ABOUT - BROADLANDS & EMBLEY PARK

EMBLEY PARK 1932 85065

belonged to the dining room, and all the rooms to the left were servants' quarters. There was a billiard room on the right, and at the back the large drawing room had views over the New Forest, which adjoins the property.

It is now a school, but was once the home of Florence Nightingale, the creator of the modern nursing profession, who came to live at Embley as a child. Her interest in nursing started very early; she is reputed to have nursed a shepherd's dog in her childhood. As a young woman, and much against her family's wishes, she spent three months at Salisbury Infirmary to train as a nurse and was horrified with the state of the hospital and the nursing staff.

By the time the Crimean War was being fought in the 1850s,

she had a decade of training behind her in various hospitals, mostly in very difficult conditions. Her work to reform the nursing facilities in the Crimean War made her famous; she became known internationally as 'the lady with the lamp'.

After the war, she successfully campaigned to make nursing a respectable profession. In order to assist military hospitals she collected statistics and made exhaustive reports, which her neighbour, Lord Palmerston, passed on to the military authorities. Her executive and organising skills were such that Queen Victoria said she wished Florence Nightingale was at the War Office. Visitors come from all over the world to visit her grave in the nearby church yard at East Wellow.

CONTRASTING ARCHITECTURAL STYLES

THE OLD THATCHED COTTAGE 1911 63784

CONTRASTING ARCHITECTURAL STYLES

The Old Thatched Cottage (63784) is a very good example of a less grand building style, one very common in earlier times. In the 19th century, generations of the Figes family brewed and sold beer here. The cottage stands in Mill Lane opposite a terrace of houses then called 'Industry Row'. At the end of Mill Lane, there were paper and corn mills, perhaps providing custom for the Old Thatched Cottage.

Until the latter part of the 19th century, brewing was done on a small local scale, but the coming of the railway and of an energetic entrepreneur changed the trade completely. In the 1870s David Faber bought one of the breweries, Strong's, not far from the Thatched Cottage. He kept the Strong name, and gradually purchased pubs and breweries, closing some and enlarging others, until the name Strong's became known nationwide and Romsey became 'Strong Country'. The Old Thatched Cottage was one of the pubs he bought; it closed in 1918.

The Manor House (see 85047 and 49339, p82) is a typical example of a prosperous late medieval family home. The later picture gives a better idea of the building style; the facing was removed in the 1920s to show the original timber framing. The building stands on the old road out of town to the south; the road is now known as Palmerston Street, but was then Southampton Road. The house belonged to the Fleming family, who were lords of the manor of Romsey Extra, until the beginning of the 19th century.

Until the nuns were removed from the Abbey in 1539, the Abbess was the lord of both the manors of Romsey Infra, the centre part of the town with its eastern boundary just beyond the Cornmarket, and Romsey Extra, the town beyond this boundary.

Priestlands School is an example of immediate post-war architecture. The Romsey School was the first purpose-built secondary school in Romsey; constructed in 1957, it was known then as Priestlands, the name of the land on which it was built — the land had been one of the properties owned by the Abbey in medieval times.

CONTRASTING ARCHITECTURAL STYLES

Unfortunately, there was already a school in Hampshire called Priestlands, so the name was changed. The First World War had prevented the building of a planned new secondary school, and the economic troubles of the 1920s and 30s again stopped the development, so this new school was very welcome when it finally arrived some 50 years after the need had first been established.

The Abbey, the Manor House and the Thatched Cottage are part of Romsey in the 21st century as they were in the 18th, when the guide book to the town mentioned that it was 'vulgarly termed Romsey in the Mud'. The corn and paper mills have been replaced by industrial estates on the outer periphery, covering a vast number of trades, including a brewery. There were only a very few years in

Romsey's history, towards the end of the 20th century, when beer was not brewed here.

The traveller of earlier days would have been unaware of Romsey's other important medieval building, standing close to the Abbey, now known as King John's House. It was rediscovered in the early 20th century, when it was part of a courtyard of small tenements. More of the town's history has been discovered in the 20th century, and care has been taken to renovate and maintain its older buildings.

Romsey has grown, but it is still a small, friendly town; and as in the 18th century, it still lies east of the River Test.

CONTRASTING ARCHITECTURAL STYLES

Above:
THE MANOR HOUSE 1903 49339

Left:
THE MANOR HOUSE 1932 85047

The nearer two bays in the 1932 picture appear to date from the early 17th century, but the smaller third bay is thought to be a century earlier. At the time these pictures were taken, the Manor House was occupied by the Ward family, who were 'Corn and Coal Merchants and Household Removers'. The 17th-century part is now a restaurant.

Below:
PRIESTLANDS SCHOOL c1965 R53053

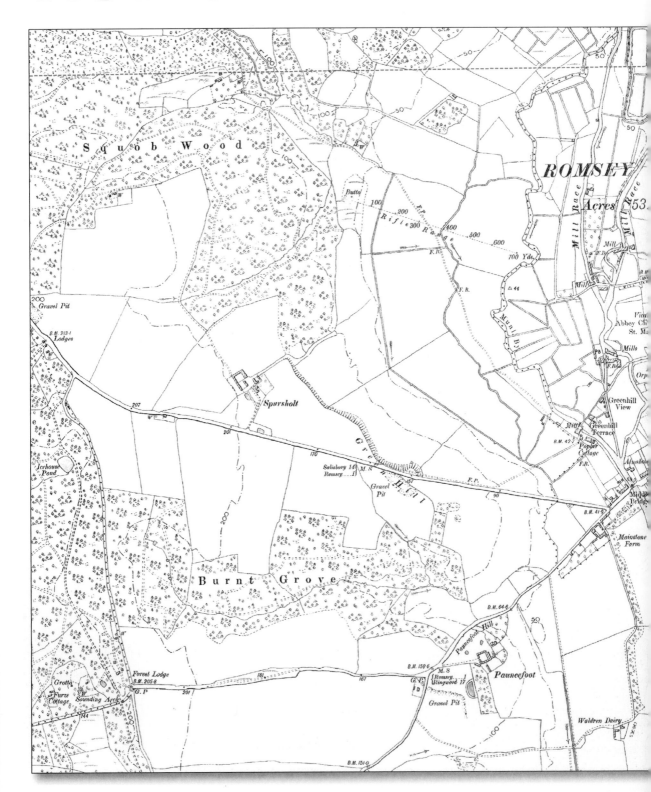

ORDNANCE SURVEY MAP SHOWING ROMSEY AND SURROUNDING AREAS 1895

The following people have kindly supported this book by purchasing limited edition copies prior to publication.

G N & R J Adcock, Romsey
To Andy Anderson, always my rock when I needed you most
Deirdre Anderson (nee Mansell)
To Annick & Yves from Lou & Vera 2005
Percy Austin, ex Romsonian
The Babey Family, Romsey
Martin Bagley, Romsey
Liz & Barry Bailey, to mark 25 years, Romsey
Robert John Baker
To our daughter Rose Lynne & Mike Baker
Phil & Julie Ball
Mr & Mrs R Bartlett from all the family
The Bartletts of Whitenap
Barbara & Douglas Bell, Bere Regis
Peter, Pauline & Nicola Belton, Romsey
To Betty, Happy Birthday
Mr D Bibby, Romsey
Irene Blake, Romsey
The Bratcher Family, Romsey
The Brewer Family, Romsey
'A wonderful place to retire to',
    A & J Brightman
A J Brooks, Romsey, 70th Birthday May 2005
Mrs Tessa F Buck, Romsey
Tony & Jo Bundy and Family of Romsey
Mr Derek Burnett, Romsey, a special thank you
Mr & Mrs D Burrell, Romsey
In memory of R F & A Dade of Bossington
1st Wedding Anniversary - Susan & Alan Dale
Callum Davey, Romsey
David & Ruth
David & Carol of Oakmount, Whitenap Lane
Diana Davies, Romsey
Rowland Davies
Brian Dawkins, Romsey
Christopher Dawkins, Romsey
Diane Dawkins
Valerie & Norman Dawkins of Romsey
Wilfred Dawkins
Sally L Dickens, Romsey
In memory of the Doe Family
Joan & Reg Dowling, true Romsonians
The Dunleavey & Alldred Families
Joan Dunleavey & the Capell Family,
    Romsey

Peter Edna & Mark Davis, Romsey
The Emery Family, Romsey
Valerie Etwell, Romsey
The Fielder Family, Romsey
Sheila Ford, Nursling
Mum, Jan Fox, love always Sharon and David
The Francis Family, West Wellow
Mr & Mrs B Fry & Family, Romsey
David Fry
Pamela Gale, Romsey - Town Mayor
    1982-1984
Fred & Maureen Gilroy
Nigel Godwin, founder of C & G Fencing
    Manufacturers Ltd, Romsey
Harry Gower, Romsey
To Russel Griffin
Carolyn & Philip Griffiths of Romsey
Mr F J & Mrs A J Gritt, Romsey
Michael M Hannah, Romsey
The Harper Family
Danny F Harrington, Romsey
Nigel G Harrington, Romsey
Jenn & Graham Hawken, 'Special parents',
    Sue x
Brian W Hillary on your birthday
Steve Hosking, 1st job Nat West, Romsey
In memory of Pauline Humber, Romsey,
    PPAPS
Mr & Mrs A Hurst, Awbridge
Lucy Hurst, North Baddesley, Southampton
Philip Hurst, Rothesay, NB, Canada
Reginald Hurst, Romsey, Hants
Lawrence H Irish, Romsey
Barbara Jeves, Banning St, Romsey
Terry & Wendy Kew, Romsey
Carol & John King, Romsey
Robert & Sara Lamb
Mr & Mrs P Larkin & Family, Romsey
John Light, Finesse of Romsey
Roy Light, Romsey
Lily Maher/Liz Kemp
Frank Martin, Romsey
In memory of R S & M A J Masters, Romsey
W J Mettyer, Romsey
Michael Edward Middleton, Romsey
    04/02/33 ex Hampshire Regiment
Marion Moncur, Romsey
The Moody Family, with love, Josie
Jane Mudge, born in Romsey 1944

To Mum & Dad from Rich, Irene & the girls
To Mum love from Steve
Shaun J O'Brien, Romsey
Sheila Parker, Romsey
Mr P J & Mrs M L Parsons, Romsey
Stephen M Payne, Romsey
Eve & Peter Phippen, The Harrage, Romsey
Richard & Elizabeth Pratt, Romsey
Tim Pratt from R & E Pratt, Romsey
Mr & Mrs B J Read, Romsey
Carl Roberts
Memory of the Rogers Family, Michelmersh
Romsey Advertiser
Joan Rozenberg-Summers, Romsey
The Shears Family, Romsey
Mr C & Mrs S Sherman & Family, Romsey
The Slocombe Family, Romsey
Peter Smetham
Bill & Norah Smewing
Nicola & Lester Smith, Romsey
Southern Evening Echo
The Stocker Family, Romsey
John & Jean Stone, Romsey
Mary & Roger Street of Romsey, Hants
The Tasker Family, Romsey
L E Tasker, Romsey
Kathleen & Glyn Taylor, Romsey
S & D Taylor on their 10th Wedding
    Anniversary
Rex & Geraldine Trayhorne, 'Romsey, a very
    special place in our lives'
Paul 'Archie' Viney & Family, Romsey
Mr Brian J Welch & Mrs Jacqueline Welch,
    Romsey
In memory of Helen Wetherall of Romsey
Memories of A & G White, late of Embley
    Park
In memory of G A Whitfield of Romsey
The Whittingham Family, Romsey
Mr J M Williams, In memory of Colin
The Young Family, Romsey

INDEX

The Francis Frith Collection Titles

www.francisfrith.co.uk

The Francis Frith Collection publishes over 100 new titles each year. A selection of those currently available is listed below. For latest catalogue please contact The Francis Frith Collection. **Town Books** 96 pages, approximately 75 photos. **County and Themed Books** 128 pages, approximately 135 photos (unless specified). All titles hardback with laminated case and jacket, except those indicated pb (paperback)

Available from your local bookshop or from the publisher

The Francis Frith Collection Titles (continued)

Lancaster, Morecombe and Heysham Pocket Album
Leeds PA
Leicester
Leicestershire
Lincolnshire Living Memoires
Lincolnshire Pocket Album
Liverpool and Merseyside
London PA
Ludlow
Maidenhead
Maidstone
Malmesbury
Manchester PA
Marlborough
Matlock
Merseyside Living Memories
Nantwich and Crewe
New Forest
Newbury Living Memories
Newquay to St Ives
North Devon Living Memories
North London
North Wales
North Yorkshire
Northamptonshire
Northumberland
Northwich
Nottingham
Nottinghamshire PA
Oakham
Odiham Then and Now
Oxford Pocket Album
Oxfordshire
Padstow
Pembrokeshire
Penzance
Petersfield Then and Now
Plymouth
Poole and Sandbanks
Preston PA
Ramsgate Old and New
Reading Pocket Album
Redditch Living Memories
Redhill to Reigate
Rhondda Valley Living Mems
Richmond
Ringwood
Rochdale
Romford PA
Salisbury PA
Scotland
Scottish Castles
Sevenoaks and Tonbridge
Sheffield and South Yorkshire PA
Shropshire
Somerset
South Devon Coast
South Devon Living Memories
South East London
Southampton PA
Southend PA

Southport
Southwold to Aldeburgh
Stourbridge Living Memories
Stratford upon Avon
Stroud
Suffolk
Suffolk PA
Surrey Living Memories
Sussex
Sutton
Swanage and Purbeck
Swansea Pocket Album
Swindon Living Memories
Taunton
Teignmouth
Tenby and Saundersfoot
Tiverton
Torbay
Truro
Uppingham
Villages of Kent
Villages of Surrey
Villages of Sussex PA
Wakefield and the Five Towns Living Memories
Warrington
Warwick
Warwickshire PA
Wellingborough Living Memories
Wells
Welsh Castles
West Midlands PA
West Wiltshire Towns
West Yorkshire
Weston-super-Mare
Weymouth
Widnes and Runcorn
Wiltshire Churches
Wiltshire Living memories
Wiltshire PA
Wimborne
Winchester PA
Windermere
Windsor
Wirral
Wokingham and Bracknell
Woodbridge
Worcester
Worcestershire
Worcestershire Living Memories
Wyre Forest
York PA
Yorkshire
Yorkshire Coastal Memories
Yorkshire Dales
Yorkshire Revisited

See Frith books on the internet at www.francisfrith.co.uk

FRITH PRODUCTS & SERVICES

Francis Frith would doubtless be pleased to know that the pioneering publishing venture he started in 1860 still continues today. Over a hundred and forty years later, The Francis Frith Collection continues in the same innovative tradition and is now one of the foremost publishers of vintage photographs in the world. Some of the current activities include:

Interior Decoration

Today Frith's photographs can be seen framed and as giant wall murals in thousands of pubs, restaurants, hotels, banks, retail stores and other public buildings throughout the country. In every case they enhance the unique local atmosphere of the places they depict and provide reminders of gentler days in an increasingly busy and frenetic world.

Product Promotions

Frith products are used by many major companies to promote the sales of their own products or to reinforce their own history and heritage. Frith promotions have been used by Hovis bread, Courage beers, Scots Porage Oats, Colman's mustard, Cadbury's foods, Mellow Birds coffee, Dunhill pipe tobacco, Guinness, and Bulmer's Cider.

Genealogy and Family History

As the interest in family history and roots grows world-wide, more and more people are turning to Frith's photographs of Great Britain for images of the towns, villages and streets where their ancestors lived; and, of course, photographs of the churches and chapels where their ancestors were christened, married and buried are an essential part of every genealogy tree and family album.

Frith Products

All Frith photographs are available Framed or just as Mounted Prints and Posters (size 23 x 16 inches). These may be ordered from the address below. From time to time other products - Address Books, Calendars, Table Mats, etc - are available.

The Internet

Already ninety thousand Frith photographs can be viewed and purchased on the internet through the Frith websites and a myriad of partner sites.

For more detailed information on Frith companies and products, look at these sites:

www.francisfrith.co.uk
www.francisfrith.com
(for North American visitors)

See the complete list of Frith Books at:

www.francisfrith.co.uk

This web site is regularly updated with the latest list of publications from The Francis Frith Collection. If you wish to buy books relating to another part of the country that your local bookshop does not stock, you may purchase on-line.

For further information, trade, or author enquiries please contact us at the address below:
The Francis Frith Collection, Frith's Barn, Teffont, Salisbury, Wiltshire, England SP3 5QP.
Tel: +44 (0)1722 716 376 Fax: +44 (0)1722 716 881 Email: sales@francisfrith.co.uk

See Frith books on the internet at www.francisfrith.co.uk

FREE PRINT OF YOUR CHOICE

Mounted Print
Overall size 14 x 11 inches (355 x 280mm)

Choose any Frith photograph in this book.
Simply complete the Voucher opposite and return it with your remittance for £2.25 (to cover postage and handling) and we will print the photograph of your choice in SEPIA (size 11 x 8 inches) and supply it in a cream mount with a burgundy rule line (overall size 14 x 11 inches).
Please note: photographs with a reference number starting with a "Z" are not Frith photographs and cannot be supplied under this offer.
Offer valid for delivery to one UK address only.

PLUS: Order additional Mounted Prints at HALF PRICE - £7.49 each (normally £14.99)
If you would like to order more Frith prints from this book, possibly as gifts for friends and family, you can buy them at half price (with no additional postage and handling costs).

PLUS: Have your Mounted Prints framed
For an extra £14.95 per print you can have your mounted print(s) framed in an elegant polished wood and gilt moulding, overall size 16 x 13 inches (no additional postage and handling required).

IMPORTANT!

These special prices are only available if you use this form to order . You must use the ORIGINAL VOUCHER on this page (no copies permitted). We can only despatch to one UK address. This offer cannot be combined with any other offer.

Send completed Voucher form to:
The Francis Frith Collection, Frith's Barn, Teffont, Salisbury, Wiltshire SP3 5QP

CHOOSE A PHOTOGRAPH FROM THIS BOOK

Voucher for **FREE** *and Reduced Price Frith Prints*

Please do not photocopy this voucher. Only the original is valid, so please fill it in, cut it out and return it to us with your order.

Picture ref no	Page no	Qty	Mounted @ £7.49	Framed + £14.95	Total Cost £
		1	Free of charge*	£	£
			£7.49	£	£
			£7.49	£	£
			£7.49	£	£
			£7.49	£	£
			£7.49	£	£

Please allow 28 days for delivery. Offer available to one UK address only

* Post & handling	£2.25
Total Order Cost	£

Title of this book . . . .

I enclose a cheque/postal order for £ . . . .
made payable to 'The Francis Frith Collection'

OR please debit my Mastercard / Visa / Maestro / Amex card, details below

Card Number

Issue No (Maestro only)   Valid from (Maestro)

Expires   Signature

Name Mr/Mrs/Ms . . . .

Address . . . .

. . . .

. . . .

. . . . Postcode . . . .

Daytime Tel No . . . .

Email . . . .

1-85937-962-1   Valid to 31/12/07

Free Print – see overleaf

Would you like to find out more about Francis Frith?

We have recently recruited some entertaining speakers who are happy to visit local groups, clubs and societies to give an illustrated talk documenting Frith's travels and photographs. If you are a member of such a group and are interested in hosting a presentation, we would love to hear from you.

Our speakers bring with them a small selection of our local town and county books, together with sample prints. They are happy to take orders. A small proportion of the order value is donated to the group who have hosted the presentation. The talks are therefore an excellent way of fundraising for small groups and societies.

Can you help us with information about any of the Frith photographs in this book?

We are gradually compiling an historical record for each of the photographs in the Frith archive. It is always fascinating to find out the names of the people shown in the pictures, as well as insights into the shops, buildings and other features depicted.

If you recognize anyone in the photographs in this book, or if you have information not already included in the author's caption, do let us know. We would love to hear from you, and will try to publish it in future books or articles.

Our production team

Frith books are produced by a small dedicated team at offices in the converted Grade II listed 18th-century barn at Teffont near Salisbury, illustrated above. Most have worked with the Frith Collection for many years. All have in common one quality: they have a passion for the Frith Collection. The team is constantly expanding, but currently includes:

Paul Baron, Phillip Brennan, Jason Buck, John Buck, Ruth Butler, Heather Crisp, David Davies, Louis du Mont, Isobel Hall, Lucy Hart, Julian Hight, Peter Horne, James Kinnear, Karen Kinnear, Tina Leary, Stuart Login, David Marsh, Lesley-Ann Millard, Sue Molloy, Glenda Morgan, Wayne Morgan, Sarah Roberts, Kate Rotondetto, Dean Scource, Eliza Sackett, Terence Sackett, Sandra Sampson, Adrian Sanders, Sandra Sanger, Julia Skinner, Miles Smith, Lewis Taylor, Shelley Tolcher, Lorraine Tuck, David Turner, Amanita Wainwright and Ricky Williams.